Pebble® Plus
Bilingüe/Bilingual

GENTE DE LAS FUERZAS ARMADAS DE EE.UU./PEOPLE OF THE U.S. ARMED FORCES

MARINEROS
DE LA ARMADA DE EE.UU.

SAILORS
OF THE U.S. NAVY

por/by Jennifer Reed

Editora consultora/Consulting Editor: Gail Saunders-Smith, PhD

CAPSTONE PRESS
a capstone imprint

Pebble Plus is published by Capstone Press,
151 Good Counsel Drive, P.O. Box 669, Mankato, Minnesota 56002.
www.capstonepub.com

Books published by Capstone Press are manufactured with paper
containing at least 10 percent post-consumer waste.

Library of Congress Cataloging-in-Publication Data
Reed, Jennifer, 1967–
  [Sailors of the U.S. Navy. Spanish & English]
  Marineros de la Armada de EE.UU. / por Jennifer Reed =
Sailors of the U.S. Navy / by Jennifer Reed.
     p. cm.—(Pebble Plus bilingüe. Gente de las fuerzas armadas de EE.UU. =
Pebble Plus bilingual. People of the armed forces)
  Includes index.
  Summary: "A brief introduction to a sailor's life in the Navy, including training, jobs, and life after service—in both
English and Spanish"—Provided by publisher.
  ISBN 978-1-4296-6117-1 (library binding)
  1. United States. Navy—Juvenile literature. 2. Sailors—United States—Juvenile literature. I. Title. II. Title: Marineros
de la Armada de Estados Unidos. III. Title: Sailors of the U.S. Navy. IV. Title: Sailors of the United States Navy.
VA58.4.R43817 2011
359.3'30973—dc22   2010041504

Editorial Credits
Gillia Olson, editor; Strictly Spanish, translation services; Renée T. Doyle, designer; Danielle Ceminsky,
     bilingual book designer; Laura Manthe, production specialist

Photo Credits
Capstone Press/Karon Dubke, 21
Defense Imagery, 5
Shutterstock/RCPPHOTO, 22–23
U.S. Navy Photo by Jeff Doty, 17; by MC2 Nathan Laird, 10; by MC3 Ann Marie Lazarek, 11; by MC3 Kyle Gahlau,
     15; by MC3 Richard Waite, 19; by MCSN Kyle D. Gahlau, cover; by Mr. Scott A. Thornbloom, 7; by PH3 Kitt
     Amaritnant, 13; by PHC Eric A. Clement, 9

Artistic Effects
iStockphoto/walrusmail (rivets), cover, 1
Shutterstock/Jitloac (rope), 2–3, 24

Capstone Press thanks Dr. Sarandis Papadopoulos, Naval Historian, for his assistance with this book.

Note to Parents and Teachers

The *Gente de las Fuerzas Armadas de EE.UU./People of the U.S. Armed Forces* series supports
national science standards related to science, technology, and society. This book describes and
illustrates sailors of the U.S. Navy in both English and Spanish. The images support early readers
in understanding the text. The repetition of words and phrases helps early readers learn new
words. This book also introduces early readers to subject-specific vocabulary words, which are
defined in the Glossary section. Early readers may need assistance to read some words and to
use the Table of Contents, Glossary, Internet Sites, and Index sections of the book.

Printed in the United States of America in North Mankato, Minnesota.
092010   005933CGS11

Table of Contents

Tabla de contenidos

Joining the Navy

Men and women join the United States Navy to protect the country. They guard oceans and waterways around the world.

Unirse a la Armada

Hombres y mujeres se unen a la Armada de Estados Unidos para proteger al país. Ellos custodian los océanos y las rutas marítimas en todo el mundo.

Recruits have basic training for eight weeks. They exercise and learn about ships. They learn to fight fires.

Los reclutas reciben entrenamiento básico durante ocho semanas. Ellos hacen ejercicios y aprenden acerca de barcos. Ellos aprenden a combatir incendios.

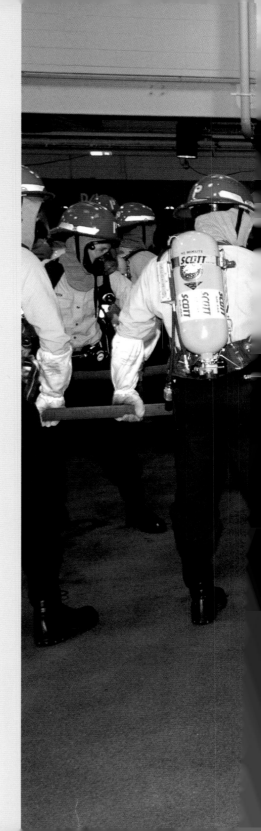

Job Training

After basic training, recruits become sailors. Next, they train for their jobs. Helmsmen steer ships.

Entrenamiento para el trabajo

Después del entrenamiento básico, los reclutas se convierten en marineros. Luego se entrenan para sus trabajos. Los timoneles conducen los barcos.

Gunner's mates work with missiles and guns. They also take care of the equipment that fires these weapons.

Los artilleros trabajan con misiles y cañones. Ellos también cuidan el equipamiento que dispara estas armas.

Navy pilots fly F/A-18 Hornets. Directors guide pilots and planes on the decks of aircraft carriers.

Los pilotos de la Armada vuelan F/A-18 Hornets. Los directores guían a los pilotos y a los aviones en las plataformas de los portaaviones.

F/A-18 Hornet

Director

Living in the Navy

Navy sailors see the world.
Many live on ships for six months
at a time. Aircraft carriers
can hold 5,500 sailors.

Vivir en la Armada

Los marineros de la Armada ven
el mundo. Muchos viven en barcos
durante seis meses por vez.
Los portaaviones pueden llevar
5,500 marineros.

Sailors who are not at sea
live and work on naval bases.
Bases have stores, homes,
and hospitals.

Los marineros que no están en
el mar viven y trabajan en bases
navales. Las bases tienen tiendas,
casas y hospitales.

Serving the Country

Most sailors serve for four years. Some sailors stay in the Navy for 20 years or more.

Servir al país

La mayoría de los marineros sirve durante cuatro años. Algunos marineros permanecen en la Armada durante 20 años o más.

After serving four years, sailors may leave the Navy. Some go to college. Others use their training and skills in civilian jobs.

Después de servir durante cuatro años, los marineros pueden irse de la Armada. Algunos van a la universidad. Otros usan su entrenamiento y sus destrezas en trabajos de civiles.

Glossary

aircraft carrier—a warship with a large flat deck where aircraft take off and land

base—an area run by the military where people serving in the military live and military supplies are stored

basic training—the first training period for people who join the military

civilian—a person who is not in the military

missile—a weapon that is fired at a target to blow it up

recruit—a person who has just joined the military

Internet Sites

FactHound offers a safe, fun way to find Internet sites related to this book. All of the sites on FactHound have been researched by our staff.

Here's all you do:

Visit *www.facthound.com*

Type in this code: 9781429661171

Super-cool stuff! Check out projects, games and lots more at **www.capstonekids.com**

22

Glosario

la base—un área administrada por las Fuerzas Armadas donde vive la gente en servicio y donde se almacenan los suministros militares

civil—una persona que no está en las Fuerzas Armadas

el entrenamiento básico—el primer período de entrenamiento para quienes se unen a la Fuerzas Armadas

el misil—un arma que es disparada a un objetivo para hacerlo explotar

el portaaviones—una nave de guerra con una gran plataforma plana donde los aviones aterrizan y despegan

el recluta—una persona que recién se unió a las fuerzas Armadas

Sitios de Internet

FactHound brinda una forma segura y divertida de encontrar sitios de Internet relacionados con este libro. Todos los sitios en FactHound han sido investigados por nuestro personal.

Esto es todo lo que tienes que hacer:

Visita *www.facthound.com*

Ingresa este código: 9781429661171

¡Algo súper divertido! Hay proyectos, juegos y mucho más en www.capstonekids.com

23

Index

Índice